THE LONG GRASS

SAINT JULIAN PRESS

POETRY

OTHER BOOKS BY LISA RHOADES

Strange Gravity
Into Grace (chapbook)

PRAISE for THE LONG GRASS

Lisa Rhoades's *The Long Grass* is the poetry of a feminist woman of faith, whose poetic fire was rekindled after the sudden early death of a close friend. These poems are of a piece with her earlier book, *Strange Gravity*, yet they represent another vision, another music that is at once calm and urgent, and absolutely breathtaking, carrying us with her, as Emerson says, "into that region where the air is music, we hear those primal warblings, and attempt to write them down." Her work breathes in the air that is music, even as it sings the question "Why must the damaged world / impinge on this November day?" Her warblings include the domestic, the realities of losses and the mundane that perhaps depart from Emerson's lofty and masculine idealism: "I want to write something exquisite / and tender, but those are not the words at hand. The words / at hand are mismatched socks, lint, and dog hair, / homework, and the flu." *The Long Grass* is liturgical; her wanting "the ornamental plums in bloom a little longer, / so everyone has time to see them / before their blousy fall" is redemption, practicing our returning to grace. Lisa Rhoades's poems are the haunting psalms of our difficult days.

—Aliki Barnstone, Poet Laureate of Missouri
Author of *Dear God, Dear Dr. Heartbreak* and *Dwelling*

"Even if all that's left / is a harvest no one bothers to gather—. . . even if it feels / impossible to find sweetness here, / still, some people can, and do." So ends Lisa Rhoades's wonderful, affirmative book in which she does just that: finds the sweet in the sour, the light in the dark, the joy in the sorrow, the love in the loss, the life in the death. Often adopting the persona of Demeter to her daughter's Persephone, she counters the losses endemic to our broken lives—beset by climate change, childhood abuse, gender stereotype and inequity, death itself—with the reassuring persistence of the natural world and the enduring promise of human love. If her motherly "worry scurries and gnaws, won't shoo away;" if the end of her daughter's childhood "looks like a snagged sweater," if grief, hunger, and rage beset us; if the dead fill our "coat pockets / with the smooth stones of their names;" Rhoades embraces "songs / of praise and gratitude." As with the pastries she dreams of in "In the bright world Demeter walks through the winter," so with her formally nimble and seemingly effortless poems: "when she flicks her fingers, sweetness rains / from her hands."

—Ron Wallace
Author of *For Dear Life*

The Long Grass reveals an urban landscape by way of its fecund gaps, the precious flashes of oaks and jonquils and the corresponding moments of connection between a daughter and her mother. I'm astonished at how the two perspectives on growth and change are both shared and disparate. "The long grass is mown but not yet raked," the title poem says, invoking Whitman's graves of cut grass, but highlighting not just the scythe to come but the chastisement we experience throughout life. We are made conscious of accruing personal losses—hardening arteries, ringing ears, degenerating lenses—in poems seemingly occupied with larger vantages: torture across the world, nearly missed connections, addiction in a daily commute, cancer in remission. Rhoades is equally adept at ecstatic odes, full of word play and joy, that deepen these complicated looks at our crowded existences. Our guide along the way is Demeter, the protagonist of a sequence plaited throughout this collection, who reminds us of the lively gods we are and all that we cannot be.

—Martha Serpas
Author of *The Dirty Side of the Storm*

"In the bright world" of the twenty-first century, the goddess, Demeter, commutes on the Staten Island Ferry. She notices a boy addict, gives coins to a woman, "...who sits / legs outstretched on a pile of cardboard with a cardboard sign," and prays for "Reverend Billy," who "...gets worked up for the Lord / in a morning routine about being saved..." At home, she struggles to raise her own son, and the daughter, whose presence from birth to adolescence encompasses the book's narrative, "The daughter rushes to be born, to break / her mother's orbit, / only to return to the circle of her arms." A richness in coming round, in the cycle of the seasons, and the complex orbits of mother and daughter, make *The Long Grass* a book to read swiftly - perhaps in one sitting - and then to read more closely a second time, with even greater pleasure.

—Victoria Hallerman
Author of *The Aerialist*

THE LONG GRASS

Poems

by

Lisa Rhoades

SAINT JULIAN PRESS
HOUSTON

Published by
SAINT JULIAN PRESS, Inc.
2053 Cortlandt, Suite 200
Houston, Texas 77008

www.saintjulianpress.com

COPYRIGHT © 2020
TWO THOUSAND AND TWENTY
©Lisa Rhoades

ISBN-13: 978-1-7320542-8-8
ISBN: 1-7320542-8-2
Library of Congress Control Number: 2019941134

Excerpts from *The Homeric Hymn to Demeter Translation, Commentary and Interpretive Essays*, edited by Helene P. Foley, Princeton University Press, 1993, reprinted by permission of Princeton University Press.

Cover Art: Elli Tzalopoulou Barnstone, *Light in the Olive Grove*
Cover Design: Marybeth Rivera
Author Photo: Marybeth Rivera

For Bonnie and Charlie

CONTENTS

THE LONG GRASS

THE DAUGHTER   3

LATE SPRING ODE   4

ERRAND   5

A SMALL MOMENT   6

YARD SONNET   7

NO   8

MOURNING SONG   9

IN THE BRIGHT WORLD DEMETER WORKS IN THE YARD   10

BEFORE I COULD SAY NO   11

POPPY   12

THE MOTHER   13

IN THE BRIGHT WORLD DEMETER FINDS A BIRD   14

SPRING BEAUTY BEAUTY   15

THE LONG GRASS   16

THE SEAM THAT RUNS THROUGH EVERYTHING

IN THE BRIGHT WORLD DEMETER WISHES   19

THE BEACH IN A SMALL SEA OF BIRDS   20

THE SEAM THAT RUNS THROUGH EVERYTHING   21

THE MASTER   22

IN THE BRIGHT WORLD DEMETER TRIED TO TEACH HER DAUGHTER 23

IN A FIELD OF SUCH SNOW 24

IN THE BRIGHT WORLD DEMETER THINKS IT STARTED WITH THE STICK AND POKE TATTOO 25

IN THE BRIGHT WORLD DEMETER TURNS ON THE NEWS 26

WORDS AT HAND 27

OUTSIDE THE VERIZON STORE 28

PRAYER STATIONS 29

IN THE BRIGHT WORLD DEMETER TAKES THE DOWNTOWN 6 31

THE HEART SAYING IT'S OK

HOW AM I? 35

IT DEPENDS 36

WHEN I VISITED AFTER HIS DEATH 37

DEAR HEART 38

THE YEAR THAT WHAT WAS LOST GOT FOUND 40

GOOD DOG 41

IN THE BRIGHT WORLD DEMETER HATES TO ADMIT IT 42

GIVE ME A KISS 43

THE HEART SAYING IT'S OK 44

THIS BOY 45

WINDFALL

MY BRIGADOON 49

THE MARK, 1931   50

CINNAMON AND APPLES   51

IN THE BRIGHT WORLD DEMETER WALKS THROUGH THE WINTER   52

AS IF ON A JOURNEY   53

THE MOST BEAUTIFUL MIGRAINE IN THE WORLD   54

BUT ALSO, THE RAIN   55

FLOODPLAIN   56

FALSE SPRING   57

WINDFALL   58

IN THE BRIGHT WORLD, CODA: THE MOTHER TELLS HER DAUGHTER   59

ACKNOWLEDGMENTS

NOTES

THE LONG GRASS

THE DAUGHTER

Every year satellites wobble and fall, flare
like a match tip and disappear,
but most junk in space
stays in space
despite Earth's gravitational pull.
The daughter rushes to be born, to break
her mother's orbit,
only to return to the circle of her arms.
They stare at each other
across the breast's warm globe—
one's eyes deep evening blue,
the other's, full of stars.

LATE SPRING ODE

O Star-of-Bethlehem, summer
snowflake, Ornithogalum Umbellatum.
O bright thing, waxy and white! O
six-petaled flowers on branched open clusters,
thumb sized and naked in tufts and clumps
throughout my yard late April and early May,
horticulturists suggest I weed you in bunches
while the season is cool, and after a rain,
collecting all the moony white bulblets
orbiting each parent bulb.

O lovely nuisance, o clever
inedible Mediterranean traveller,
winter lily's odorless, toxic cousin,
I applaud your resistance to herbicides,
your arching grass-like leaves marked midrib
with white, and drooping unlike Allium.
How you are everywhere and then gone,
like waves of foam following a boat.
How you open and shut with daylight and dark
like a small boy's hand. Your names evoke
all our dreams and frustrations:
someone named you "bird's milk"!
but also, "dove's dung." Someone
looked at a ten-inch multi-flowered spike
and saw a way to Christ, a midwinter's journey.
O field onion, O Arabian Star!

Your South African name sounds
like the Spanish word for bed bug
Tjenkenrientjee, Chincherinchee, Chinche.
Weak-stemmed, a florist's nightmare, you don't cut well,
a problem calcium chelators can minimize,
but who would bother for a difficult weed.
Hurrah for having escaped cultivation, for
shouldering in and hunkering down during the hottest days.
O Wonder Flower, Grass Lily, the Nap at Noon.

ERRAND

Let me stand here. And let me pretend I see all this...
　　　　　　　　　　　　CP Cavafy

The leaves refuse to change this year, and fall
instead in heaps of brown. Everyone blames
August's long drought, September's, as well—
months of the weathermen gloating
"another mild weekend ahead"—
without mentioning global warming.

In the back seat, Bonnie keeps watch
and a running tally of the view:
"I see a boat. I see the moon."
Manhattan deepens in purple across the harbor.
"Shiny city!" she exclaims.
Dark water, darkening sky.
We drive Richmond Terrace
toward the ferry terminal. Long-empty lots
now under construction—
years of weedy abandon ending
in concrete and condos. I try to see
"without blurring the beauty with loss."
Not all the trees have disappeared.
It will take more than her lifetime for these
waters to rise. My girl wears a blue
hat her grandmother crocheted,
keeps pointing, ecstatic, into the air.
I make out "Princess, Castle, Birds."
I pretend I see it all.

A SMALL MOMENT
after Cornelius Eady

I huff up the stairs, worried
I'll miss my boat. Across the plaza,
a beautiful boy with dark curls
lurks. He is here every morning
begging. He asks everyone who passes
for the bus fare home.
Dressed in the clothes of the life he is leaving—
deep red chinos, deck shoes, a plaid Polo—
he twirls into my path with a sheepish
"how'd I end up here?"

When I say a small prayer that he
be released from his addiction,
when I wonder how his parents
carry their worry, I am shouldering
the work with my fellow commuters
who also shake their heads
and shrug out of his way.

The days are shorter, darkening.
It is early October, a few days until
the first hard frost. He bows
like a courtier in my direction,
his skin red and shiny as a potato.
Our breath lifts in small clouds.

YARD SONNET

We go out almost every afternoon
into the yard. While Bonnie shrieks and runs
today, a helicopter churns the blue
above the house, incessant, and a sign

of trouble somewhere. I keep raking leaves—
huge roach-brown oak, and then the maple's gold,
the small sumac's red—thinking, "Please, please, please
just stop it now." Why must the damaged world

impinge on this November day? Its pull
is constant. Sirens break into the night
and rupture dreams. I won't deny that all
of human loss and love are her birthright,

I just want more of this: my darling girl
safe in the yard. She chases leaves and birds.

NO

No with a sigh, pleading, flung out with arms
and kicking.

No with weeping and giant tears on her lashes,
her hands tight and tangled in her tangled hair.

Broken *no* of exhaustion; silent *no* of betrayal—
As I hold her for the doctor, a limp *no*

followed by moaning. *No* to the blue pants, the corduroys,
the sweet flowered boots, to waffles and 32 oz. of milk.

No panties. Not ever. I never, never, ever
panties. Testing *no* and its new partner,

Stop. From the back seat please *stop.*
No white food! *No* green! But then

No to the tune of Happy Birthday to You. *No*,
I'm not kidding. Sing along, I know you can:

NO, NO, NO, NO, NO, NOOOOO
as she runs laughing and naked down the hall.

MOURNING SONG

The mourning doves on Serifos
chant "Let's have sex! Let's
have sex! Let's have sex!"
as if a teenager with a megaphone
were standing below the balcony,
or so my friend recalls. While she tells
the story, the birds start up and soon
so do our girls—laughing and cavorting
in a breathless flush of SEX, SEX, SEX,
a word they know enough to know
has swelled the room with pleasure.
And how far into the future will they carry
this memory of their mothers,
who are themselves bursting
with memories as they dance
in bras and pj bottoms?
One day soon, the little one will see
something she will later recall
as her earliest memory—the way
the older insists she remembers "a man
in a blue suit standing next to dad."
And what about this poem, itself
a small bird calling a low *wuh hoo, hoo, hoo,*
as it rushes toward the future's
empty wind-swept rooms?

IN THE BRIGHT WORLD DEMETER WORKS IN THE YARD

She bends the jonquils to the ground
and they bounce back and forth in response.
The hostas' curled tongues are up,
and the newly seeded grass casts
a light green across the bald yard.
Everywhere, the work of her hand:
hours tending and pruning, and starting
from seed, and everywhere the work
undone. Her trowel rings
in the soil and brings up a porcelain doll head,
thimble-small and grubbed with dirt.
Nearby, her daughter builds a teepee for her Barbies,
clipping branchlings from branches
with a pair of old loppers, wild haired and singing.

BEFORE I COULD SAY NO

1.
At the Monastery of Archangels the chapel's Madonna smiles
above an altar brimming with Tamatas, pressed tin
and pewter tokens—limbs, and hearts, and eyes—
anything that can break, anything that can be healed.

I offer her my worry, a small animal
I tuck among the petitions
and pray it scuffles a new nest
away from the dark warmth of my heart.

Back outside, Father Makarios closes the bright blue door
against the midday heat; laundry twirls from balconies.
"Come here, come here my joy" he gestures to my girl,
who beelines to the rosewater sweets he offers her.

Beneath ancient fruit and olive trees, she chews quietly.
Radiant, sugar-lipped child.

2.
Radiant, sugar lipped child
chewing quietly under the trees,

you had your hand deep in the box of candy the old priest offered
before I could say no. He said your secret name aloud
and I dizzied in the midday heat. Shirts waved from balconies.
A blue door closed.

My heart is cluttered with broken things. Broken things
and hunger. Worry scurries and gnaws, won't shoo away.
It fattens with my happiness. I cannot let it go.
I try to let it go.

Anything can be healed. Anything that can break:
limbs, hearts and eyes. The altar brims
with petitions and prayers, beneath the smiling Madonna
in the chapel at the Monastery of Archangels.

POPPY

When she comes to you holding
the poppy—the strange single blossom
that showed up beneath the bird feeder
its stalk a stiffened piece of twine
just within sight of the kitchen window
where you leaned not so long ago
in front of a sink of filthy dishes and marveled
that it hadn't yet been trampled by the goddamned new dog,
because that was the kind of morning
it turned out to be: another crappy morning
of dirty dishes, a whining child
the dog harassing the neighbors over the fence
and you glanced up and saw
a bright blossom, a small prayer you
closed your mind around and so
you didn't yell or hit or break
well, *anything*. That poppy.
When she comes to you holding
that poppy, saying "I picked this
for you," hold out your hands
for the shocked and dying flower
its black center like a swollen bee and say,
thank you, thank you, thank you, thank you.

THE MOTHER

Where is the mother of this mother
who nightly lets her child cry herself to sleep?

Who gave her the book that says this is right?
What does she do as the crying wears on?

Why was she given such a stingy, sullen girl,
small house, small life, small child with her alone?

Twenty-one in suburban Kansas without a car,
she rinses breakfast plates before the yolks congeal.

From the crib a rustle, another morning nap ending.
She thinks maybe she'll make meatloaf for dinner,

with a canned pear slice adrift on iceberg lettuce,
and a dollop of mayonnaise, poised.

How far would she get if she had the De Soto?
She puts on her girdle, some stockings. It is time to set out lunch.

IN THE BRIGHT WORLD DEMETER FINDS A BIRD

— a feathered dot,
almond brown—
on the sidewalk. She means to save it,
to set it in a tree,
but sees its scissored beak—
how it will starve, and soon,
so she takes it to the vet
who suggests ether's kindness
and she agrees
to have it killed this way. She leaves
the small bird in the metal cage
and walks out into the sun
and the fall-struck trees.
"Better than being crushed" she thinks,
but not by much.

SPRING BEAUTY BEAUTY

Beside the Ralph's on Victory Boulevard
sits the Spring Beauty Beauty nail salon,
with windows decorated by placards
to advertise the work I could have done—

a facial, deep massage, or pedicure—
by young Korean girls whose downcast eyes
are practiced, inscrutable, and ensure
the promising illusion that I might

get up from their care—nails lacquered, hair curled—
and be young again. Firm. But not today.
Instead, I'm eating ices with my girl,
and it's ok I'm old. I watch the way

the willow green ice cream runs down her wrist:
this child, herself a blossom, daisy dressed.

THE LONG GRASS

The long grass is mown.
The long grass is mown but not yet raked.
The cut stalks interlace and dry in a net
above the green.

Everything is green.
Everything is green and slightly sour.
The girls gallop and gallop, pretending
they have horses.

The girls gallop. They are horses.
They run the field of red clover
and rye—inflorescence
above; a sweetness within.

Everything is sweet
Everything is sweet and slightly green.
At the bottom of the trough, pale algae waves.
They run the pump to fill the tank. They dip their faces in the cold.

By summer's end they are bored and tan.
By summer's end they are young women.
Right now they wander to Salem Free Church
to weave graveyard flowers into their manes.

THE SEAM THAT RUNS THROUGH EVERYTHING

IN THE BRIGHT WORLD DEMETER WISHES

all oranges were blood oranges—
the magenta-tinged skin hinting
of darker cells below, how orange
and not orange they are. The luxury
of cultivars, of orchards and vineyards
travelling the small slope of a hill and a life
spent tending such gifts. The cool evenings
necessary for the trees to thrive. Now everything
can be had, and none of it tastes good.
Each morning her daughter leaves in darkness,
shoulders a backpack and disappears
into the city for school.
Sometimes Demeter stands in the room,
touches the warm sheets from which the girl arose,
sometimes she carries that longing all day.

THE BEACH IN A SMALL SEA OF BIRDS

House sparrows and finches drift
between the feeder and leggy rose
outside the kitchen window.
Back and forth they riot, this dun flock
of everyday birds, consuming
all the seed—black sunflower and thistle,
the cracked corn and millet,
leaving nothing for songbirds.
Some days, something brilliant
surfaces in the otherwise brown—
the crisp white stripes
of a chipping sparrow's head—
and just as quickly disappears.
In the surge and retreat of their hunger,
I stand washing dishes—
the beach in a small sea of birds.

THE SEAM THAT RUNS THROUGH EVERYTHING

climbs from the wrist,
a vein meandering to the heart;

the way a hoodie drawstring twists
with earbud wires toward a pocket, and the rails go on, end to end
across their perpendicular ties;

it stumbles through the subway car muttering
"everything sucks man, everything bro"
a lanky sorrow bringing a gut-chill with its nearness;

or it is Japanese knot weed and invasive, hollow
stemmed and determined, and the life spent digging it
from the yard;

it slices through a friendship, the wet edge
of the trowel; it gets up early to walk the property line
straightening the poles, tightening the barbed wire;

until it surfaces in East Blue Hill to travel
the pine-y edge of Curtis Cove
as a scar-white slash across the granite ledge
just above the water line,

where I span the cursive "from there" and "to here" of it
with my body on a towel.

THE MASTER

Jesus, Peter, James and John
go up to a mountain, which is not named.
Jesus disappears and comes back after some days
face shining, in glory, garments white as the light,
and Peter says "Master, it is good for us to be here.
I'll build you three tents if you want to stay."

So many of our fathers had
a "master of the house" thing going on—
a set of rules to be obeyed, dinner ready
when they came home.
My dad would spank me with a leather belt he'd pull
through his pant loops as he walked the hall
to my room, where I was crying before he got to me.
You better believe I did my best to be good, first for him,
and then for every man in charge,
all those proxies—my father,
the scout master, the night manager at Wendy's, one
professor after another, drunk
or not, at parties,
or not.

Our black priest doesn't flinch
at using "master"—I do.
Why tarnish the mountaintop moment—
Christ revealed to all as God by God?
Why "master" when "rabbi" or "teacher" is true?

Then again, I forgave my dad years ago. Most
of the other men, too, though sometimes I'll revise
the memory from 10th grade
when Luanne and I had to swim extra laps for being girls.
I have us emerge from the deep end,
faces shining, in glory,
and I make the coach say "good job," to us
like he did to all the boys,
instead of "give me four more
just to be sure you can."

IN THE BRIGHT WORLD DEMETER TRIED TO TEACH HER DAUGHTER

caution, tried when she was young,
to show her simple rules to keep
girls safe—no earbuds on the bus,
keep your midriff covered and your distance
from angry people and fools.
In the end, it didn't matter—
he climbed through her bedroom window,
he groped her on the crowded train. He
told her every other girl had done it
to get the job. He uploaded her pictures,
chained her to the radiator, locked her in the office,
pushed her down behind the dumpster. He gave her drugs
meant for horses so she could not
move or scream. He took her into custody,
he took her by the hand, he told her he'd be gentle, he tore her
shirt from her breast. He told her she didn't deserve
better. He beat her and addicted her and sold her
to his friends. He picked her out from the larger group
and followed her from school. He raped her
while her parents chanted prayers in the next room.
"With his horses Hades snatched her screaming
into the misty gloom."
She was slut-shamed by her friends. It was all her fault.

IN A FIELD OF SUCH SNOW

This morning my girl let me braid her hair, draw
the brush along her crown and reveal
the white-pink of a part through ash brown waves,
while she sat and sobbed. The morning had been torn
in two by sad news. She cried, and the morning
was torn in two. Tears traced her cheeks.
Beneath my hands, her hair was smooth.
I folded it over and under itself.

The end of her childhood looks like a snagged sweater—
an unraveling that might be slowed but not stopped—
or the branch I can see from my kitchen window,
thick near the trunk it twists to join
the lace on lace of neighboring limbs
as they arch away and out of view.

Outside a wet snow falls and melts, travels the gutters,
and runs down the hill, drawn to the Kill Van Kull.
But there are places where snow falls and stays,
grainy and too heavy to blow away,
where the past presses against the deep past,
until a glacier is formed.

In a field of such snow, this filament,
this sadness slender and strong, would melt into
the history of mornings and refreeze
with every moment of every year before and to come.
My hands release the weight of her hair,
she packs up her book bag, and disappears.

IN THE BRIGHT WORLD DEMETER THINKS IT STARTED WITH THE STICK AND POKE TATTOO

her daughter gave herself at camp one summer,
bored and unsupervised,
with self-loathing tent mates. Harpies,
they blew through the girl's good sense and spent
the afternoons passing a needle
and small vial of ink between them, giggling.
Her daughter jumped with each prick but continued
stabbing her skin with methodical precision
until five small numbers emerged on her heel,
this "trim-ankled maiden" of song.
And for the Gods' sakes, numbers!
As if the girl could not read
the world around her, couldn't remember
all she had learned of the past. Every incarnation
of this story fills with grief and rage.
Demeter searches the internet for pictures
of infected homemade tattoos, bubbling
with pus and the hot pink of eaten flesh,
and sends them to the girl,
along with Connecticut State statutes
outlining the crime of tattooing a minor,
or providing the materials for them to do it themselves.
"How long will you keep bringing this up?" her daughter
groans. "You know me," Demeter replies.

IN THE BRIGHT WORLD DEMETER TURNS ON THE NEWS

and the lamentations rise: #bringbackourgirls—

"I have a daughter out there, without shoes."

"Is it nothing to you, all you who pass by?
Look around and see."

"I was raped every day. How am I telling you this
without crying? I tell you I ran out of tears."

"She did not consider her future. Her fall was astounding;
there was none to comfort her."

"No one re-chews a piece of gum. You throw it away.
And that's how easy it is to feel like you no longer have worth…
why would it even be worth screaming out?"

In her grief, hunger. In her rage, the winter
light. The valleys between her knuckles deepen.
In the window, a candle burns day and night
until her daughter's remains are found.

"I heard her voice throbbing through the barren air
as if she were suffering violence."

The Nigerian government confirmed 110 girls are missing
after suspected Boko Haram militants attacked a school in the
northeast, the largest abduction since Boko Haram kidnapped
276 girls from their school in Chibok almost four years ago.

"The mountain peaks and the depths of the sea echoed
in response to her divine voice, and her goddess mother heard."

"I want to die, because I'm missing my daughter Leah Sharibu.
She is a good girl-o. She likes school. I never sleep, I never eat."

Bella was then taken to the hospital and was pronounced dead.

Her lost girl; in the bright world, #metoo.

WORDS AT HAND

I want to write something exquisite
and tender, but those are not the words at hand. The words
at hand are mismatched socks, lint, and dog hair,
homework, and the flu.

I want the pigeons
out of my yard. They bully the smaller birds—
the male cardinals hopping along behind their mates to feed them.
I want the bellies of the females filled.

I don't want the words MOAB, refugee, and rape,
unemployment or cancer to grow sticky
in the lives they invade.

I don't want to be petty about my desires,
or worry about money in the presence of my wealth.
I want big things, too, and not just for me:
shelter and prayer, friends

meeting in the street with a hug,
the ornamental plums in bloom a little longer,
so everyone has time to see them
before their blousy fall.

OUTSIDE THE VERIZON STORE

Army green but wicking yellow
from ruffled skirt to spine,
all the gingko leaves dropped last night
as the weather snapped,
and the season finally changed.

In blue-pink evening light, a cabbie
pulls to the curb on 3rd Avenue
and sets out a small green rug between
the street light pole
and free newspaper box
to dip his head in prayer.

Uptown being mostly East, despite
being at the top
of every subway map,
it makes sense, geographically, to face
the Verizon Store and say Allahu Akbar.
God is great, God is good.
Witness: to the leaves,
as they swirl in small spirals
at the gutter, to the lowering light,
to the man who is praying,
and to those who don't
break their stride.

PRAYER STATIONS

When the Prayer Stations erupt with leaflets and collection cups
alongside the street vendors hawking NYPD baseball caps,
incense, small bags of candies and nuts,
and America's religious take their place—
God and commerce mixing it up
with grief—at Ground Zero, I think about
the drive-through Daiquiri Huts
of my Louisiana youth—convenience
being the true church of my age—and there was nothing
more amazing at 18 than to have
32 ounces of rum and crushed ice, sweet and dangerous
passed through the open window of a late 70's Cutlass.

   *

Amazing, too, that I survived that time
and what came after—at 35 still drinking,
but so much more by then, and dating
first this one married to someone else, then that
one addicted to cocaine, divorced myself as well.
One night on the Pulaski Skyway headed
from Jersey City toward the Bayonne Bridge,
I threw a glass limned with bourbon from my car.
Liberty's backside and the mass of the city
shimmered over my shoulder.

   *

Each spring, St. Nicholas parishioners
mark the Stations of the Cross
by marching down the street in song and penitence.
The kids dressed up as guards have whips
they get to crack and pop
toward the one boy dressed as Christ.
I love Good Friday for the comfort
of grief—the cindered snow still piled on the corner
and the crocus and jonquils pushing themselves
through dog crap and garbage and the hard
knot of dirt, for the weeping at a funeral
and the meal that follows—the way we must
get on with it, even as afternoon darkens.

   *

To marry someone who's kind,
to whom you can say "let's go home" and they will
leave the party to find your coat on the bed,
is to let luck bring you to long mornings of sweet regard,
but the story of salvation is not without work—
the pilgrimage ends with a long walk home;
the morning moon's pearl edge dissolves
inexorably toward the sun.

*

On the Staten Island Ferry, Reverend Billy
gets worked up for the Lord
in a morning routine about being saved
from kidney failure
"so's to preach the evils of Adam and Steve"—
an abomination his god couldn't possibly have conceived—
for commuters congregated at the front of the boat.
Some mornings I manage small prayers of my own:
Bless this man in his anger and fear.
Witness the body he believes was broken, is healed.
For those who don't bother to lift their heads
as he rants, a benediction: you will finish your coffee
before we get to Manhattan.
Let the women in the Ladies Lounge blink
in mascara'd satisfaction
through the difficulties of their day. Bless the man
selling bootleg CDs, the other selling shoe shines
guaranteed to "get you a raise." And those who are quiet
and alone. Keep the lovers pressed into each other at the railing.
Lift up the American Legion churning across the harbor,
the ones sitting outside facing Brooklyn in late fall
closing their eyes against the sun.

IN THE BRIGHT WORLD DEMETER TAKES THE DOWNTOWN 6

walking past the homeless woman who sits
legs outstretched on a pile of cardboard with a cardboard sign,
between the staircases to the platform.
Sometimes she is crying and slovenly. Sometimes
she looks clean. Sometimes a small boy sits with her.
Sometimes Demeter gives her change. The coins slip
from her fingers, alien as stone.
She'd rather hand out bread, a cup of coffee, or soup,
but she recognizes hunger that can't be met.
She thinks of her daughter's school projects over the years,
the creative whirl at a kitchen table covered
in oak tag and markers, scissors and tape,
the pencil smudged finger tips,
the holy smell of girl lifting from her crown
as she hunches over
the most important task in the world.
Arbitrary, and by this she means
not "highhanded" or "capricious" but
"without reason."
She assumes they find the cardboard
outside of the bodegas, or liquor stores, or groceries.
But what about the markers? The thick permanent ones
aren't cheap.

THE HEART SAYING IT'S OK

HOW AM I?

How am I? This time it's the sitter who asks. How am I? How am I to answer her? How much does she know? How am I to keep track of whom I've told your cancer has come back? How long until you are sick again? How many months of chemo this time?

How do we go back to that waiting room, its tasteful earth tones, free coffee and graham crackers? How am I going to occupy myself there? How many novels can one person read? How many overheard murmurs of hope and loss does it take to ruin one lovely fall afternoon? How am I to watch, and wait? How is this happening again? How not to blame you for being sick—how not to shame you for not taking better care, how not to read the ropey scars on your chest like a Dear Lisa letter full of betrayal and your plans to leave. Or more: a rebuke to how much I'll let you suffer just as long as you're alive?

How do I tell the kids cancer will chaperone every soccer game and prom? How do we fix everything wrong between us? Desire's chasm and the ugly fight we keep having. And on the subject of fixing, how about the sidewalk, heaving up like an old grave after a storm, the slipping shingles, the wagon's weak power steering: how am I to make this work if you're dead?

How not to make dark jokes about dying? How about this one: I don't want to bury that man unless I get to hit him over the head with the shovel first? How can that not be funny if you know us? How can it not be sad? How do I answer people who admire how I am coping? How do I wait to grieve until you are gone?

IT DEPENDS

We are all sick. We are all dying.
This is more or less
the truth, depending on the day.
Depending on the location,
some more than others
are headed home with hospice, toward
a tragic confrontation, a chicken bone, black ice.
Maybe it's because of breakfast—
years of bitter coffee, the eggs
we were warned away from,
bracelets of sweet cereal "o"s.
Perhaps it would help
if more of us knew CPR,
unless it all depends
on the weather of our hearts.
Don't be fooled
by how quickly flesh folds
back into itself to heal,
or by the ones who are limping,
waxy skinned and quiet. They will not carry
your part of this forever.
Maybe you should cover your cough,
not be so careless with knives.

WHEN I VISITED AFTER HIS DEATH

When I visited after his death,
I slept in my friend's father's room
on a small hard mattress,
which was not where he'd died.
That had happened in the den
in a rented hospital bed
dismantled soon after his body
was removed. In the bathroom
the clutter of dying remained:
pink plastic basins, disposable pads,
ointments and small sponges to wet his lips.

This was in a city I'd left years before
so I drove to all the places I knew,
sat in the small shade of a crape myrtle,
taking pictures of grey herons
fishing the shallows, and pelicans
bunched up on logs.
It's not the first time I've felt
useless to people I love—

The night before I left
we went bra shopping at the mall,
just a little drunk. We let
no nonsense clerks
tuck our breasts
into lace and spandex
as we laughed.
On her own she found
a black dress, and wrote his Eulogy
and I suppose cleaned up
what I could not,
including the Mylar
"Get Well" balloons
adrift near his dresser.

DEAR HEART,

> *"The sweet spot in life to get off the couch and start exercising*
> *is in late middle age when the heart still has plasticity.*
> *You may not be able to reverse the aging of the vessels if you wait.*
> Dr. Ben Levine, AHA journal, Circulation*

oh, pinched heart,
tight and full
as a skirt that once fit,
bunched up
with all the sadness
I can find, I know
you thought you'd seen the worst—
years of thumping along
toward one bad choice
or another—the boy in 7th grade
who kissed Nanette instead,
the gay boys who kept us around
for their moms, even
the sad professor, the lost marriage—
all the sorry places I put you.

Now the news tells me you're growing
smaller and stiffer with age, a rubber band
in the bottom of the drawer,
both brittle *and* slack, which might explain
how so many moments burst
with grief. The party
my son wasn't invited to,
the other mother's back peddling,
lame excuse. Small potatoes
in the workings of the world,
but it doesn't need to be big for me
to cling to it too long.
My friend is trying to forget
Polar bears—their emaciated bodies
on the news, the map
of their shrinking world, her sorrow
for them too much to hold.

There's a fix, of course,
and it doesn't sound like fun—
not gardening or the stretch of travel,
meditation or prayer.
Only "moderate to high intensity
aerobic exercise
for four or more days a week"
can turn back the clock.
And what would I do
with a thirty-five-year-old heart
but break it again and again?

THE YEAR THAT WHAT WAS LOST GOT FOUND

It started early enough: the five
pounds I lost in January returned
in February before my birthday.
When one orange honey comb-patterned glove
disappeared, first I got back the memory
of the Toronto store on Queen Street
where I'd found the pair
and a calamari-curled scarf to match, and with that,
the satisfying extravagance of their purchase
with Christmas cash from my grandmother
came flooding forward twenty years
until a friend admitted she'd seen it
in the shrub beside her porch
and thought it might be her sister-in-law's,
at which point I retrieved
the actual glove as well.

Bonnie, at seven, kept working her tongue
beneath one milk tooth after another
until she lost them all and the new ones
brought with them a lovely gap
she said she wanted braces to fix.
An estranged friend visited
and talked happily of his son's
engagement while I served tea and
even though it was just a dream,
his face didn't melt or my mouth fill
with ants, so I woke up happy
and glad for him the next day.
So when the black designer coat
the dry-clean manager suggested
might be in my car as I clawed through
hundreds of hissing plastic bags
showed up in my husband's closet,
I found a way to hold my tongue.

GOOD DOG
for Dana

The boy says, "No,
I said, go," but the brindle bitch
can't stop herself, hang-tailed
with her longing she squirms
in his direction; her teats brushing
the fallen leaves.

She wants him so badly
she grovels into traffic—
a blue truck swerves—
the boy snaps his wrist up and hard.
Good dog, she shudders
back to the broken curb.
"Not his no more,"
his friend shrugs,
explaining what only she can't see.

She'll have nothing
of my soft "hey girl;"
she won't be saved by me.
And how would that work anyway?
Her straining against me, dreaming
of him? His baritone's
the only signifier she'll behave.

Leaves obscure deep cracks
in the pavement; I catch myself
before I fall. He is just a boy.
She is just a dog.
Some of us can't see our riches.
And some of us can't see them
until they are gone.

IN THE BRIGHT WORLD DEMETER HATES TO ADMIT IT

but she loves pop songs from the 80's,
wishes the hymnist had had a synthesizer
back in the day.
She's particularly fond of Pat Benatar—
the oracular quality of a Juilliard-bound Coloratura,
who becomes a singing waitress instead.
Demeter has burned bridges like that before.
Sometimes when she was young, her daughter
would sing along with Demeter
when a song they both knew came on the radio.
In such a way, one day could be lit within.
"We belong to the night, we belong to the thunder."
Talk about a tribute, even Zeus would love that one.
Who needs slaughtered goats and lambs?

GIVE ME A KISS

"Here" I say to my sadness,
here is a beautiful day.
Let's sit together on the fishing pier
and close our eyes to the small *pffts* of cloud,
to the old man doing calisthenics
on the bench next to us,
picking up his leg, picking up
his arm, again and again.
Vigorous. Exhausting just to watch.
Let's feel pathetic for a minute. Now,
isn't that nice?

Isn't it nice, just the two of us—
having ice cream for lunch? Driving
until we come to the beach
to sit, head tilted toward the sun,
as a boy cuts big hunks of bait
and laughs with friends
about the shark he will catch,
sluicing guts and blood in ribbons
toward the drain and the dark water
below the dock, where a small sand shark
moves closer to entering
the boy's bragging heart.
If you want, we can think about
laundry and dishes, the undone to-do list,
that angry letter, or our dead friend.
Whatever you want; I'm all yours today.
Don't be shy, take my hand. Give me a kiss.

THE HEART SAYING IT'S OK

Everywhere, fountains of apricot and dun: Royal Elk, and Canna,
the Yucca's yellow-centered star. All the reaching-up plants
reach up before falling down.

Simple enough, some days, to trumpet my good luck.
Look here! Look here: a woman with friends, coffee
in a cup the size of a bowl, everything generous and large.

Simple enough to look the other way,
to wake up small-hearted and sad. What hurts, hurts hard.
The math is simple in the economy of loss.

In the coffee house: a couple wearing flannel shirts and sturdy shoes.
What will be the measure of their day? He gets up, she says
"don't stay long." Their kiss a stitch, their love a seam.

Sparrows cling to Pampas grass in the warm lee of a building:
the bricks hot with the afternoon sun, the birds flickering and full.

A small list: groceries, letters, the dishes filling the sink.
What will get crossed off? What will remain?

The body taking up the effort. The heart saying it's ok.

A bright flair against the sky, the glassy lake,
the still-green, October trumpets orange.
Trumpets red. Trumpets fall.

THIS BOY

Sometimes on his way into sleep,
Charlie twists
a handful of my hair
through his fingers and holds tight
until he casts off from this mooring
into his dream. Through the night
he is a restless boat,
journeying across the mattress to his dad
and back to me,
a restless boat that stills
when anchored
with the sleep-deepened weight
of his hand to my back.

One day he will drift
into his own bed,
this boy who was bullied
in the spring of last year, who
called himself "the extra part
in the machine that works the world,"
this boy who has engineered
an intact family in the darkest
moment of our marriage
as we reach out to touch across him,
as we each take his hand.

WINDFALL

MY BRIGADOON

> *A musical by Lerner and Loewe, Brigadoon*
> *is the story of two tourists who stumble upon*
> *a village that appears for only one day every 100 years.*

The small town in me surfaces
when I enter my aunt's rural church
where the mothers and girls
sit to one side,
and it's sweet smelling and soft there
as we sing "on that beautiful shore
The melodious songs of the blessed;
And our spirits shall sorrow no more,
Not a sigh for the blessing of rest."

In the church hall sharing a meal—
meatloaf, macaroni, and slaw, airy
yeast rolls, berry crumble and cake—
it's easy to lose track of time
listening to my dad tell the story again
of the ten-dollar Jersey calf
he bucket-raised and later bred.
His small herd built one cow at a time
and sold to pay for college.

I know the day will end. I know
that when I leave, my cousins,
softening and grey, with grandchildren spilling
into the yard, will wave me on
toward Highway 19 across
the Warm Fork's deep pool
where communal baptisms were held
when dad was a boy, and beyond
the Ozark foothills and bluffs
through the lowlands outside Jonesboro
where nearly all the state's rivers flow
into the Mississippi, an alluvial plain
of stripped cotton fields, as the sun sets
and I make my way home.

THE MARK, 1931

As a child she couldn't find it—the mark
she knew was there, somewhere.
She'd crane her neck to peer
at the trellis and gate post and above
the dark slash of canker growing
part way up the tree. Each day
she examined each deeply
for the smallest charcoal smudge,
she searched for drag marks through the gravel
in the alley behind their yard.

Once she found two stacked twigs
and read it as a sign
pointing to the porch door vined in roses.
How else did they know to come
to her house
hat slapped into their palm,
asking for odd jobs, these
able-bodied men trying to trade
work for food, day upon day?
Her mother would send her
from the kitchen with butter on bread,
a baked potato, or piece of meat,
maybe cheese,
wrapped in waxed paper,
not much but no one had much,
for her to hand to a man just like her dad,
a railroad engineer by trade,
who in a nearby office
(she later knew) was letting
his employees go
one by one.

CINNAMON AND APPLES

To sit with the dying
in this nursing home, a series
of widows and grandmothers cycle
through 5 hour shifts working for Hospice.
In knit pants and sweaters, with quilted bags
of yarn and needles at their feet,
or Suduko books tucked
beside them in the chair,
good Christian women
supplement poor retirement accounts
by witnessing my mother's grief
and my grandmother's rough breathing
while oxygen shushes on.
For a while, the room smells
of cinnamon and apples, the uneaten cake
on the bedside table and of a body
shutting down. Hospice is here
for three people this weekend:
the gentleman in 406 dies first,
followed by the lady in 210,
as my beloved grandmother lives on
through another shift at work
for Audrey, Lynn, Joanne,
Audrey again, Lynn again,
Audrey at the end.

IN THE BRIGHT WORLD DEMETER WALKS THROUGH THE WINTER

wearing a big coat that looks like fur
but is really some form of tightly spun plastic,
or petroleum, or fiber, she's never been sure,
but it keeps her warm. This morning
she decides to eat oatmeal—she spoons it
from a cardboard cup while waiting
for the Ferry. The terminal fills with commuters.
She remembers when Charon was young
and not mad, the silky blue of his eyes—
how they sparked when he worked, and how happily
he worked, skimming the river of woe.
He'd hate it here, but feel at home
in this waiting room the size of the world.
The oatmeal is gummy and warm;
she finishes before it's time to board.
Tomorrow she'll get a doughnut instead.
She's already happy thinking of the snap of fried dough
between her teeth, the flakes of sugar on her lips,
how when she flicks her fingers, sweetness rains
from her hands.

AS IF ON A JOURNEY
after Aliki Barnstone

Some days my dead crowd in, filling my coat pockets
with the smooth stones of their names.
   Gone. Gone.

I carry them with me, bundled up
and shuffling onto a boat, setting out
   as if on a journey—

But this is the Staten Island Ferry.
Most of us are weary of the commute
   before the trip has begun.

Sit down and read with me,
doze, or crochet, watch
the water behind the boat knit shut.

THE MOST BEAUTIFUL MIGRAINE IN THE WORLD

The most beautiful migraine in the world
starts like small town fireworks
dome shaped and weeping
shoots of long burning silver
as I look across a darkening sky.

All the dogs start barking
to answer the bangs and reports,
the whistles and whumps that match
my tinnitis, my heart.

The whole world's abuzz. It glistens
like sunlight through a hat's woven brim,
with sprays of sparks, no tails
or trails, overtaking the small shadows
that normally cross my view.

After the small-scale pyrotechnics—
the Crossettes and Chrysanthemums,
the Roman Candles and Diadems—
the scattering of applause,
people head up from the beach.
Flashlights stutter along the path
to the cottage. Everything softens.
The last bottle rockets fiz and pop,
I close my eyes to the smoke and the stars.

BUT ALSO, THE RAIN

The lens of the eye, they say, yellows
with age, and tends to absorb
and scatter blue light—

the way picture glass wears
a sticky nicotine tinge
long after the smoker has quit,

in other words, maybe it's just for me
the sky and river blend
in dusky grey. Ravishing.

Lavender. But also the rain
pulls the horizon
into the middle of the East River

closing the harbor mouth
with an ashy screen. My cab speeds
down the FDR, while taillights glint a warning

no lovers ever heed:
no matter how close two people seem
—nothing separated her rain swept-skin from mine—

darkness eventually defines
what a thing it is to be so bound.

FLOODPLAIN

In vesper light I drive
Arkansas lowlands
north toward Missouri
and a funeral.

For miles, the horizon
thins
to a reddish thread
beyond cotton fields
lining the road.

Alone in a small rental
I careen
past river-laced land—all
that's been dragged
this far.
Dusk builds
toward night.

Beside the highway until
the tracks and road
diverge, a train
flickers. Along
the ditch
unpicked bolls cling
to plum stalks the harvester
missed.

The hour requires songs
of praise and gratitude
and I try.
From the damp
and temperate air
mist rises
into fog.

FALSE SPRING

It's true each February holds
at least one thaw that sends us
to the backyard in light jackets
to gather downed limbs
from the big tree to burn,
and survey the work left over from fall.
We can't stop ourselves from cleaning up,
bruising as we do tender perennial shoots in the melt,
doing to ourselves the same, exposing
what we love to storms yet to come.
So it happens this year, too, except
one warm day turns into five,
a false spring after a winter
that never fully arrived
and the lavender crocuses planted
by the owners before us,
small cupped and pale, push
through the crumbling leaves,
and the city's newly planted cherry
and ornamental plum
fall for it too, and bloom.

WINDFALL
for Liz

Even if all that's left
is a harvest no one bothers to gather—
wild apples softening in the brambled ditch
of a two-lane country road,
bitter little fists pocked by
codling moths, dented
and browning in the August sun,
and the work seems thankless
and lonely: too much time
rinsing and peeling, separating
rot from flesh, and even if it feels
impossible to find sweetness here,
still, some people can, and do.

IN THE BRIGHT WORLD, A CODA: THE MOTHER TELLS HER DAUGHTER

she's writing a poem
in which the mother is the earth goddess.
"So I've got some power here."
The daughter responds, laughing and kissing
her mother's brow.
And this is the sweetness of their love
in a nutshell, as they say, the meaty fear
in the mother's heart,
and this is how they crack
even when happy together,
because the mother is saying "you will suffer
and be lost,"
and the daughter hears
"I am a goddess, too."

ACKNOWLEDGMENTS

Grateful acknowledgement to the journals and anthologies in which these poems appeared, or will appear, often in different form:

Barrow Street: "Poppy,"
Beech Street Review: "The Heart Saying it's OK,"
Big City Lit: "Mourning Song," "Yard Sonnet,"
Like Light: 25 Years of Poetry & Prose by Bright Hill Poets and Writers: "Before I Could Say No," "False Spring,"
Green Briar Review: "The Mark,"
Hospital Drive, the Literary Magazine of the UVA School of Medicine: "Give Me a Kiss,"
Literary Mama: "No,"
New Ohio Review: "It Depends,"
Poetry East: "Late Spring Ode," "The Daughter,"
Prime Number Magazine: "Windfall,"
Saint Katherine Review: "Outside the Verizon Store,"
The Same: "Errand,"
Saranac Review: "My Brigadoon," "In a Field of Such Snow,"
Smartish Pace: "The Long Grass,"
South Carolina Review: "The Most Beautiful Migraine in the World,"
Sweet: A Literary Confection: "Words at Hand."

Many dear and steadfast friends encouraged me through the years by being first readers, wise critics and gentle editors. Abiding gratitude to Dana Caulkins, Catherine Doty, Liz Howell, Kelly Linn, Sara Steen, Denise Stone, Blake Traylor, and Tracy Williams. Special thanks to Michael Carman, Robert Monda, Robin Locke Monda, and Victoria Hallerman for indispensable readings of early drafts. Liz Howell and Peggy McDermott provided seaside retreats where immeasurable work and reflection could take place. Johanna Gilbert helped me with a big decision. Deep appreciation and love to Aliki Barnstone who helped guide the shape of the manuscript and never gave up on it, or me. Thank you, Martha Serpas for all that endures. David Nygard, I am glad to be on the journey with you.

Thank you Marybeth Rivera for your friendship and generosity.

Thank you, Elli Tzalopoulou Barnstone for painting *Light in the Olive Grove* and for your permission to use it here.

NOTES

"Errand": The epigraph is from C.P. Cavafy's poem, "Morning Sea."

"In the Bright World": All quotations from the *Homeric Hymn to Demeter* come from *The Homeric Hymn to Demeter Translation, Commentary and Interpretive Essays*. Edited by Helene P. Foley, Princeton University Press, 1993.

The poem refers to the myth of Demeter and Persephone which tells the story of a daughter (Persephone) given by her father (Zeus) to her uncle (Hades) in a transaction to which neither she nor her mother agreed. Demeter searched the world for her daughter only to be told that she was with Hades in the underworld. Furious at Zeus, Demeter "ordained a terrible and brutal year on the deeply fertile earth." (Foley, verse 305). Eventually, the mother and daughter were reunited, but Persephone was compelled to return for part of each year to Hades.

"In the Bright World Demeter walks through the winter": Charon is the ferryman over the River Styxx who takes souls to Hades.

"In the Bright World Demeter hates to admit it": quotes from the lyrics of *We Belong*, Pat Benatar, (1984).

"In the Bright World Demeter turns on the news": #bringbackourgirls refers to a social media campaign in response to the 2014 abduction in Chibok Nigeria of over 276 school girls by the Muslim extremist group, Boko Haram. Two weeks after the kidnapping of Polly Klaus in 1993 her mother Eve Nichol told the *Press Democrat* (Dec. 10, 1993) "I have a daughter out there—without shoes." "Is it nothing to you, all you who pass by? Look around and see" (Lamentations, 1:12). "How am I telling you this without crying? I tell you I ran out of tears" Yazidi girl speaking of being held as an Isis sex slave to *Independent.co.uk*, Monday 24 July, 2017. "She did not consider her future. Her fall was astounding; there was none to comfort her" (Lamentations 1:9). Having been raped by her captor, Elizabeth Smart recalled the destructive impact of exposure to sexual education programs *she had experienced in school in which* a sexually active girl is compared to a chewed piece of gum "Video: Elizabeth Smart Speaks, Johns Hopkins University" May 9, 2013. "I heard her voice throbbing through the barren air as if she were suffering violence" (Foley, verse 67). In February, 2018, the Nigerian government confirmed another 110 girls were kidnapped by Boko Haram (Time.com). "The mountain peaks and the depths of the sea echoed in response to her divine voice, and her goddess mother heard" (Foley verses 38-40). Three year old Bella Edwards was killed by her stepfather April 3, 2018 (newyorkcbslocal.com). #metoo refers to a social media campaign started in October, 2017 in response to allegations of sexual abuse by men in power.

"In the Bright World Demeter thinks it started with the stick and poke tattoo": "trim-ankled maiden of song" (Foley, verse 1).

"In the Bright World Demeter tried to teach her daughter": Much of this section consists of found material. Polly Klaus was kidnapped through her bedroom window in 1993. TV anchorman Matt Lauer was accused by several women of sexual assault in 2017 and was found to have a special locking mechanism on his office door. January 2015, two Stanford University students spotted a freshman thrusting his body on top of an unconscious, half-naked woman behind a dumpster. A California jury found the former student, 20-year-old Brock Allen Turner, guilty of three counts of sexual assault for which he was sentenced to six months in county jail and probation. The judge said he feared a longer sentence would have a "severe impact" on Turner, a champion swimmer who once aspired to compete in the Olympics — a point repeatedly brought up during the trial, as reported by Buzzfeed. The Bureau of Justice Statistics notes that incarcerated women are overrepresented among victims of sexual abuse given that there are far fewer women than men in prisons and jails, Amnesty International April, 25, 2017. An Indian court sentenced self-proclaimed Indian spiritual guru Asaram Bapu to life imprisonment for raping a 16-year-old girl in 2013. Asaram was found guilty of sexually assaulting a girl during a religious ceremony intended to cure her of evil spirits. The girl had been brought to Asaram by her parents, though they were not present during the time of the alleged assault. Asaram's legal team questioned the age of the girl, claiming she was not a minor and had repeated the seventh grade, CNN. "With his horses Hades snatched her screaming into the misty gloom" (Foley, verse 81).

"The Master": refers to the Transfiguration of Christ as told in the Book of Matthew.

"Words at Hand": MOAB stands for "The Mother of All Bombs."

"My Brigadoon": quotes from the lyrics of the hymn, "The Sweet By and By," Sanford F. Bennett, 1868.

"Floodplain" refers to vespers, the practice of daily evening or sunset prayers in the Anglican tradition.

ABOUT THE AUTHOR

Lisa Rhoades grew up in the Midwest and moved to New York City in 1987. She holds an MFA in Writing from Columbia University and was a Poetry Fellow at the Wisconsin Institute for Creative Writing. She is the author of *Strange Gravity*, selected by Elaine Terranova for the Bright Hill Press Poetry Award Series and published in 2004. A chapbook, *Into Grace*, was published by Riverstone Press in 2003.

Her work has been published in such journals as *The Bellingham Review*, *Chelsea*, *Pleiades*, *Poet Lore*, *Poetry East*, *Saranac Review*, and *Smartish Pace*. Before becoming a nurse, she taught at CUNY College of Staten Island, Rutgers University, and as Visiting Poet through Poets and Writers Poetry in the Branches and the Geraldine R. Dodge Foundation. She lives on Staten Island with her spouse and their two children.

Visit her Amazon author page at: *amazon.com/author/lisarhoades* and meet her at *http://lisarhoades.com*.

Typefaces Used:

TYPEFACE: PERPETUA TITLING MT – LIGHT
TYPEFACE: GOUDY OLD STYLE – Goudy

www.ingramcontent.com/pod-product-compliance
Lightning Source LLC
Chambersburg PA
CBHW080448110426
42743CB00016B/3314